songs for the dancing chicken

emily schultz

D1554782

MISFIT

ecw press

Published by ECW PRESS
2120 Queen Street East, Suite 200, Toronto, Ontario, Canada M4E 1E2

LIBRARY AND ARCHIVES CANADA CATALOGUING IN PUBLICATION
Schultz, Emily, 1974-
Songs for the dancing chicken / Emily Schultz.
Poems.
"A MisFit book".
ISBN-13: 978-1-55022-769-7
ISBN-10: 1-55022-769-6
1. Herzog, Werner, 1942– —Poetry. 1. Title.
PS8587.C5474S65 2007   C811'.54   C2006-906905-0

Editor for the press: Michael Holmes / a misFit book
Cover and Text Design: Tania Craan
Cover Image: Courtesy of Werner Herzog
Typesetting: Mary Bowness
Printing: Transcontinental

The publication of *Songs for the Dancing Chicken* has been generously supported by the Canada
Council, the Ontario Arts Council, and the Government
of Canada through the Book Publishing Industry
Development Program.

DISTRIBUTION
CANADA: Jaguar Book Group, 100 Armstrong Ave., Georgetown, ON L7G 5S4

PRINTED AND BOUND IN CANADA

ECW PRESS
ecwpress.com

for my family, and
for *Annie* and Herman Schultz

Hear the song of a chicken without a head
As it goes scratching in grave-dirt.
A song in which two parallel lines
Meet at infinity. . . .

— Charles Simic, "The Chicken Without a Head,"
Return to a Place Lit by a Glass of Milk

contents

III.   a climax of dirt

IV.   in the factory

V.   letters to heartbreak

VI.   poems for the wrong person

I

songs for the dancing chicken

I can smell death all over my fingers.
—Timothy Treadwell

Heart of Glass

Over time, grieving is as calm
as this. A colour's
forgotten recipe.

A locked cabinet contains
what will never
be produced again.

In a drinking contest no one will win,
one man says to the other, *I'll sleep off
my hangover on your corpse.*

He has the face of a lion.
The fat man and the thin man.
Both will fall.

There will be a cat in the barn with them
who won't know what to do.
I stand in the middle of the street today

and ask myself, *Where am I?*
What city is this?
Am I in a poem, or a film,

or is this dreadful traffic
part of my life? How many years
are you dead now?

The sky is the shade
of an ordinary rock glass
in the bottom of a dishpan.

New Rats

I relate to the rats, the rats that run like a river,
because I have known rats.

Those of alley eateries, now and then thieving
their way into my closets.

They've scrambled among winter boots, soiled
pages of old diaries.

In this version, they hatch from black caskets
packed solid with earth.

Even evil closes its eyes, sleeps, must sleep
in the ground where it was born.

Carried by river, this cargo eats grown men
in a solitary night.

This ship bumps to shore, brown rats rise from water,
bubbling, flooding the city.

As if a phantom is divided among a thousand incurrent
beasts, each lugs disease.

And in our own lives, how often did we avoid moving closer,
gazing into the coffins of relatives?

The bald man with long fingernails. The dirt.
And vermin.

Inside inexplicably, like necrophagous flies.
These rats.

They step over one another on supper tables,
tombs, church steps.

Colliding ghosts on ground level. The genetic similitude
of a thing

that sees by sonar, flies blind, sleeps upside-down,
and a thing

that scratches the backs of cabinets, nibbles the night,
sees with its teeth.

Fifty years before I was born, the original, *eine symphonie*
des grauens.

Even Dwarfs Started Small

A dead chicken and a live chicken on a patch of grey dirt.
The living paws at the dead with pale talons, as if to wake it
while attempting to consume it, plucking
its white-tufted feathers and swallowing.

In a bare room, an unseen director tells you which way to look:
    Are you dumb or something?
Like a mug shot, a licence plate clutched to your chest —
for you, the size of a seat from a child's swing.

    You might as well confess. We already know.
In the hall, four women and two men lined up on a bench,
wearing plaid shirts and everyday work clothes,
tough, tiny, mascaraed old girls, with sleeves rolled up,

alongside little Johnny Cashes who stare straight ahead in black
and white. There's no stare like a stare without colour.
You know what is coming for them.
You know you are just one of the others.

Herzog's Other Shoe

It is jealous of what the other one went on to prove.
Right and left, the first met and surpassed all expectations,
got itself stewed up with shallots, martyrdom, and savoury.

Twins of suede and rubber, throats of leather, the second
is Cain. Sentenced to wander alone on some desert highway.
How far can you wander, when you are just one shoe?

Do the gates open for the bone of a boot, or only
for the panting and barking tongues of distant dogs
whose graves are marked with the son's open-air guitar?

I Am Seeing a Film

I am seeing a film.

I am seeing a film
and you are with me.

I am seeing a film
and you are far from me.

I am seeing a film
and the theatre is bathed
in blue light, but the insides
of my mind are crimson.

I am seeing a film
and morality is small
as popped corn.

I am seeing a film
and thinking about story,
how it has its downfall,
how narration isn't
worth spit, because we are
able to sit in two places.

I am seeing a film
and my heart is beating.

I am seeing a film
and my retinas know
more than I do.

I am seeing a film
and I am sitting behind
myself watching myself.

I am seeing a film
and I am in France.

I am seeing a film
and I am in the American South.

I am seeing a film
and I am on the Canadian West Coast.

I am seeing a film
and I am in my parents'
living room back when it was still
the colour of apple pulp.

I am seeing a film
in a theatre where the ushers
wear costumes and I wish
I were that thin again.

I am seeing a film
and trying to record the experience
to retell at a later date,
because I want the catharsis
of having bonded to at least
one movie *so much*
that it changed my life
the instant I first saw it
and I immediately went out
and did something reckless or wonderful.

I am seeing a film
and making a list
of reckless and wonderful things.

I am seeing a film
and wishing I could press pause.

I am seeing a film,
gripped by the sudden fear
that I knew you in another life,
that when I walked across
the lobby to meet you,
we were both other people.

I am seeing a film
and the world does not belong to me.

I am seeing a film
and driving out of the city
in a car I no longer own
to a song I love
and no longer listen to.

I am seeing a film
and your mother is still alive.

I am seeing a film
and my dog is waiting
in the dark apartment
with the mice.

I am seeing a film
and Alfred Hitchcock
makes his cameo
sitting beside me.

I am seeing a film
and George Sanders leans
from the other side,
whispering sweet evil in my ear,
beneath that suave,
righteous face of his,
that face now long dead,
George Sanders' lovely suicide lips.

I am seeing a film
through Wong Kar-Wai smoke,
a 1960s smoke,
the smoke of my father
and of all fathers.

I am seeing a film
and standing atop
a sylvan precipice,
breathing Herzogian air
clouded with dirt and clamour.

I am seeing a film
and contemplating
synonyms for green.

I am seeing a film
and I am here and no place else.

I am seeing a film
and outside the cinema
it is raining, a soft slight rain,
just enough of a rain,
a rain like the wind was waiting
to use the drops
to beat a message
against the window
of a certain girl, get her attention,
so she doesn't make
that grave mistake,
but I have no idea
it has even started, this rain.

The Conquistador of the Useless

(for *Klaus Kinski*)

(1)

The fuzz of fog.
The slim outlines
of fornicating trees.

                               A thatched-roof boat
                               rowed out from the dark.
                               Horses drinking champagne.

(2)

Many children wait to watch
Fitz fall asleep
to music —

> or is it the music
> itself
> they wait to observe?

> > A closed-church face.
> > Deny religion for music, head frantic
> > as the bell tongue above.

> A child with a violin
> plays for prisoners
> and little girls.

> > The white man released
> > in his white suit.
> > Forty small hands reach to hold ice.

> A large fish
> in a man-made pond
> swallows 1000-dollar bills.

A businessman
and a businesswoman
make love among prostitutes.

(3)

The water has no hair to hold on to.
Blond face, molten heat.
Flaming mould of propeller.

> From muddy banks
> hundreds wave. Ship equipped
> with fronds and flowers.

> > *There are silences*
> > *and*
> > *silences.*

> > > The black umbrella of the dead
> > > floats on water. A hand-cranked
> > > phonograph preserves.

Shot of lit moths at night.
Blue flickered spots on the dark.
Dreams that both save and damn.

(4)

Explosions of earth.
Chaos of human toil, cloaked in brown
against a brown mountain.

      With little rope, but unlimited
      trees, vines, and physics.
      Trust.

            The man in the white suit, ankle-deep
            in mud, sits with only the earth
            and his pulley.

                Cabled hill and hull.
                The moon white as a bowl
                of yucca.

(5)

A real boat plunges down
a real mountain, in real rapids, capsizes
in real circles.

What could be
the last shot
of a failed performance.

A single empty opera chair
yawns red as hope. And in the end, anyway,
Caruso.

Sergeant Brown

It begins with a dulcet huffing,
like the distant thump of ocean, or bay
of bassoon. Why are we most beautiful
when we fight: our coats shimmering, the motion
of muscle striping arms and shoulders, agility
clear and quick as sunlight, eyes intent?

In a dance of lumbering, flat nostrils flare
moist against each other. We bark, salivate,
dig back legs deep. Our paws find their positions
as if by music. Our embrace is a joining of face,
of teeth, of haunch and claw, of shaking,
of hissing directly into one another's maws.

We force each other horizontal into sand and shit,
a ploughed-up "say uncle" hold, bury jaw into scruff-
heartbeat and jugular. Back legs thrust from below,
one foot against throat, the other against grizzly groin.
We are one circle of fur, a yin yang of brown
where white and black dots meet at the head, face-off

instead of floating separately in balance.
I am hoping your ear is your Achilles. I can come back
from the ground. I am larger than you think.
Fluff surfs through the summer air with its gulls.
Yet I cannot beat you simply by shirking your advantage.
The final steps are yours, braying low, breath in my ear.

Loss is lying flat
upon belly, before a fluttering inlet
with its crisp and unending blue line.

The Boat in the Tree

It does not need to be a real boat, but the idea
of a boat, which may be as difficult. There is no papier-mâché here:
peel your trees into planks. And place the planks in a tree.

Speak the language of scaffolding,
blisters, hammers, nails, and sweat. Truth of location,
remnant splinter. Beauty, which even as it builds,

knows it will be abandoned, washed
by three decades of equatorial rain. And still it will
exist, floating above the thickness of its island.

Build it, not on cunning water or dung earth,
but, like madmen, a hundred metres up a jungle tree:
full wooden hull, mast and sail, ghosting the Amazon air.

Aguirre is not a man, but a misery. The vessel
is cut loose of its destination, flung far from any river,
film the last trickle of silver.

Song for the Dancing Chicken

Here is Herzog, a man who would train chickens
to dance for dinner in a penny arcade. Not three seconds
but a full fifteen. Repeat and reloop. Peck that piano.

Scratch that dirt. Knock your rotten red head against the prize.
Longer, little bird. This is not a mere exercise
in entertainment. Europe understands

Americana's script is written for animals.
A kernel of corn to console you. You — stupid, cannibal
creature with cockfight proclivity — you are capable

of more. You are the most important chicken in history,
you and your chicken sisters, mysterious stand-ins
for those of us lacking fleshy claws, freckled feathers.

His film crew can call it rubbish, storm off in a huff,
and return to find that art is the stuff already happening
among the hay: harmonica, barnyard shuffle, and birdshit.

For Werner Herzog

The man
with a gun in his hand
that will bring the ending
mounts the empty
ski lift
and rises

a sign on his back
above the story

Double Double and Hell on Earth

(a stir-stick medley for my husband)

(1)

At the end of the day we listen to separate music.
We plug into our own systems, a wall apart,
ears corked with foam, sound wash, blip or fuzz.

For you, documentaries, with their click of facts.
Entire obscure albums pilfered through LimeWire.
Experimental noise. Drone. Internet radio.

For me, slow-moving fictions, rented or purchased,
and the love poems of rock singers who've committed suicide
or been murdered by steak knife, overdose, girlfriend.

(2)

But it is Herzog's voice that lulls me when I cannot sleep.
This laptop springs with music, voice, despair. German
mountain-climbs my cochlea with foreign syllables.

One night, still strung to the face of the machine, turned away, on hip
and couch cushion, I hear *Aguirre*'s theme apart. On endless loop,
the lull of its absent image: even through slumber, the sound of green.

(3)

What hems columbine clouds, fire-thick, in the abstract blue
of a grey sky? The chortle of engine and human chuckling.
Laughter, the soundtrack to cruelty.

A peewee parade who plays sticks and bells.
Runs over my typewriter — mine, you see — at least twice.
Howl, don't weep, for these bastard poems.

(4)

I am small. I didn't just start this way. You are the dwarf who laughs himself to death. I am the blind one, with his cane, and at the same time, all of his assaulters. But I will be the gasoline. You can be the flowers.

(5)

A beetle bride and a grasshopper groom, their skulls
stuck through with pins. The monkey shall dance on its cross
in anklets of string. A Senegalese song of swoon.

Riveted to games of crucifixion freeze-tag, child's squabbles
are pocket-hankied into adult clothes. Some will play school;
others will hide behind window screens, skimming photos of nudes.

(6)

Another night, Bruno S., with his large head, waits on pause,
as if contemplating his role in *Kaspar Hauser*, though here he plays both
xylophone and accordion at once, sing-shouting of faith, betrayal —

for an audience of garbage cans and windows, a hanging patch
of thin, tin sky, a gang of small boys with hoods and hats pulled low
in the damp and snow-dim confines of a concrete square.

(7)

The cattle auctioneer we experience together, marvelling, choking
at the high-speed cud-chewing of syllables that trace
with finger-haste the ribs of words, as easily as reaching out

and feeling an animal with the flat of one's palm. The action
is made inside the mouth of a man in a parka who arrives at sold beef
(or sold home) in thirty seconds. The dollars and cents of sentences

rounded down to a ding-a-ling, woodchuck-chuck, cock-a-doodle-doo
collection. Without you, I have driven through this America more times
than I can count. By the age of six I had seen a real-life dancing chicken,

a wretchedness not worth its wooden nickel. One tug of a string,
it retrieved the pellet and went back to its nest. So we live in the ass-end
of Ontario: poisoned water, but we can see a doctor for free.

(8)

On the Native reserve where your niece and nephew are being raised
the word *Indian* still hangs above the souvenir shop. In a yellow field
we take a photo of a car too defeated even for cinder blocks, and watch

Stroszek again, Thanksgiving, playing hooky from the family. Herr Scheitz
steals a turkey. The diner conversation, the teepee gift shops, are, you say,
the absolute picture of a double-double and hell on earth.

(9)

Are Herzog's animals friends? Does the mallard who beats the drum
keep time with the others? The rabbit rides a fire truck in his cage
and the piano-playing chicken pecks at keys.

(10)

Where are these things and these instruments going to end up? Bruno asked
of his baby grands, long before he rode the lift. What would happen
to them when he died? *Someone must answer this for me.*

(11)

Eva Mattes' ass, a poem on its own,
accompanied by music.
Eyes of coffee steam.

(12)

Tomorrow, corded into our work, we'll again find the tactile silence amid our unconnected noise. A wired patience, which we'll strike at, exclaiming, *Is this really me!*

II

better hell

If you go to Hell, you'll be fried chicken.
If you go to Hell, you'll be fried chicken.

— Anonymous man on the street,
Parkdale, Toronto, April 26, 2005

Better Hell

You've got nothing but your secular skin,
so don't be fooled by memory.
Your head is in cahoots with your groin.
What's in your skull, a mountain of ash.
It's not real. All you've got's the lines on your palm,
so you know better than to trade 'em
with the bucktoothed kid at recess.
One night you'll dream
the devil is sewing your legs together
while making love to you.
Don't worry your head. You're not Catholic.
Do whatever makes you feel better.
Rev your engine. You got so much to give.

You got a stack of papers tacked up on your wall.
One says *The Prodigal*. A pile of words in little rows.
Imagine a song that's got tired.
A woman who weeps into a bowl.
The way night hangs around on a street corner.
The way you sometimes make believe
your mother painted into another life, monastic,
shaving her head and wearing nothing but blue,
kneading your easy sins into bread dough
and feeding them to the other kids.
You like that sad stuff, your brother says,
jerking his thumb at the page. *Think it makes you deep.*
Yeah, why not? you say. *Hell. What else is there?*

Just Leaving Now

Smoke is only friends with the sky,
a joker with party-trick entrance.
That's what we learn from the cab
of that truck beside the 427,
crowded with the yellow wash
of flame, and you say,
Don't look. It's not respectful.
Someone could still be in there.
Even now, I can see its passenger
window rolled all the way up tight —

and the orange moved azure inside,
through upholstery, springs, plastic,
the neon-faced indicators of speed,
licking glass for leftover air, a tongue
darting out the cracks like a reverse
wire hanger, to unlock the world from inside,
black shirt still hooked to one wonky end.
The untouched gate, back, body
of the vehicle, perfect as the blue sky.

Three Layers of Night

Hell has its own sense of structure,
you dream it a hundred times
before you live there.

Three layers of night,
and the arms you once wrapped around you
shivering now.

The first layer skin;
second, bone. The third layer
only night.

Inside you, it is larval —
all your hell, waiting to hatch.
Blinking in blood, down in the dark.

An anvil falls out of the sky,
taking down little birds on its way.
Gravity outgrows its own weight:

nine days to fall
and nine days to fall through,
plummeting past red rock.

Bronze over chaos, earth and eros, then:
pull out a packet of paint chips, and choose
the colour of your misery.

Dress the inside walls of Hell's nursery.
When the anvil lands, gather it up in a baby's flannels
and use it to crush your sparrow heart.

The Man Out of Time

He puts all his hats on one head
and ducks outside, the night a blue feather
in the band of the one that went missing
years ago.

At the bar a hundred voices smoke silk,
spin to the ceiling, and no one notices the seven
stacked heads upon his noggin
though someone says:

> *You look different.*

The Problem of Diminished Joy

There are no children here.
It's part of our diminished-joy bylaw.
. . . Except that one little boy
who told his younger brother
to stick his hand inside the combine —
just to see what would happen.

But he's not much of a boy anymore.
He lived to seventeen
before exiting in a mad drunk
he keeps reliving. He teeters around
talking about the farm, the red flowers
only he can see.

If You Lived Here, You'd Be Home Now

We used to be allowed visitors on rain days
when fires were low enough to let them through . . .
but then came the reports.
The bad parents ruined it for the rest of us.
Now the only singing is the spit
of water falling on flame.

Stick around long enough
and it's a chorus of baby birds.
It's bullets sputtering in Lilliput,
or the snap of memories. Streetlights shrieking
after bedtime, and the way I once lay awake for hours
plotting my own funeral:

each rag-wrung tear, my mother's black purse,
my father's huge trembling. The caragana bush
beyond my window weeping, petals everywhere. How its hair
tossed shadows I wanted to climb into
more than any girl's.
How I cried myself to sleep with bliss.

If You Drive Like Hell, You'll Get There

You come to me at night.
Trap me in conversation at
the toilet without a cubicle.

In these dreams I'm always
like a sock left in the street.
We pint up and murder.

It's easy. We're made of newsprint.
We blow through the alleys,
wind up in the locality of my childhood,

its grey cul-de-sac ice-cream-cart bicycles,
carved jade lawns, and suppertime betrayal.
Facedown in my old neighbour's pool.

A Styrofoam beer-can holder
bobbing alongside me: comical, cool.
My only friend.

Just Before the Night Ripped Open Like a Sash

God and I are in a cabaret,
my father playing piano
with a crowbar and a candlestick —
an instant set of string drums
— beating away, seventeen in his sixty-year-old skin. *Dix minutes*
pre-curtain, Death is off having near-experiences
in the bathroom with the man they call Wilde.
When we see Death again, in his slim white
clam-diggers, he's chewing on teeth
like they're Chiclets,
yammering two octaves too high, our leading man
utterly fucked up on formaldehyde. *Quel* disaster!
Daddy-O goes *forte*, for there's no such thing
as *fortepiano* when your audience is mostly ghost
(their lives are quiet enough the rest of the time).

Onstage the painted set wobbles,
threatens to tumble
like a Warhol girl in a crêpe-paper dress.

God staggers through the hall,
meekly barters away eternal life
as he bums a smoke off a mortal,
sits in the overpowered light
of the dressing room, muttering,

Without Death, we have to cut the whole third act.
Without Death, it's the only option. . . .

In the chalky gloom,
beneath luminescent elbows,
the tabletop is globbed with glitter and rouge.
From the other room, above the smashing,
an arc of singing takes flight,
fastidious as a woman crying.

God sucks in a long breath, rewriting
sans lexis. The boas in the closet,
like live creatures, tremble.

Fume Poem

Forget the hooey. The thing here that bugs
is the heat. Like Virginia, midday,
bristling, juicy with it. The air. A raw chunk
of flesh. An after-hours armpit, sweat
goes without saying. The only sweet,
a flower at night that fills each timid
cobbled bed on the street with cotton and refuses
to be named, bleeding thick through the window,
some old ghost. 5 a.m. is the new 3 a.m.

Drive out this time of night
from Strawberry Street, west on Monument Avenue,
hit the 24-hour gas/snack at Thomson
and Ellwood, its charged green Open.
Buy two bags of Lays, one for you, one
for the person you've excreted through the day,
through the night, turning, your exile self.
Eat them to silver bag bottom before you reach
the shared rented place you call home.

Sit in the laneway beside this colonial house,
listening. Its backyard with seven roofs.
An urban hollow camping place whose solace is
its darkness, its set of parking instructions, hydrangea.
The neighbourhood hears you. It's that heat.

It climbs in you, ejects you from yourself,
crawls cockroach-quick across your skin. Nettling.
Makes you sound before you even step. Skin a red noise
in magnolia stillness. Killed ignition/air-condition.

Tomorrow, buy two hours for a dollar.
The igloo of a repertory theatre. Let your V8 rest.
The old-dog evening turns expertly over.
Keeps snoring, belly sides shaking, tongue out.
It's hot here. Hot like something you only read about.

Winter Sticking Its Tongue to a Pole

Snow has its own voice.
It swallows everything else.

It culls the click from dog toenails,
tucks it under with religious tenderness.

It eats the embers from your throat,
stills words before they are spoken.

It is propelled like a very young woman
who has removed her white brassiere,

flinging it into a corner with abandonment
she does not feel.

It says O, O, and O.
Its flakes are infinite as binary, discharging all doubt.

It falls through the night, sighing.
It seeps through the night, singing.

God does not love me, Snow says.
I am December. I am forever. I am despair.

The world wrapped in slapdash skin.
The world wrapped in methodical air.

Milk

A chorus of chocolate and strawberry cigarillos
stationed beside the cash register suddenly mute, no longer
wafting their illicit scents into my susceptible non-smoker's nose.
Only newsprint now, and stale licorice, a last cellophaned snack cake
bloated on the counter. In the rack where its friends sat, only price tags.
Dust bends over the calculator. The ghost of last month's owner.

Its new marshals have already forgone formality: delivery.
This lapsed convenience store, yawning, toothy white. In dreams I cross
the pulsing turbulent street to reach it, my tongue tight with ambition
for soda pop/pop rocks/potato chips — trauma. This site instantly
transformed to discontent. A depot designed to sell emptiness,
bleakness in paper or plastic. Its endless lintless shelves. A litany to
    bungles.

The clerk's mono-vocabulary, a gibbous pause preceding each article,
No . . . no . . . no. . . . O odious lamentations, so frequent even my papillae
have learned to sing the out-of-stock refrain! Garbage bags, bagels,
dish soap, Scope, lemonade, Dutch Maid, an elegy to Pedigree and kibble.
Tonic? . . . No. Matches? . . . No. Faded coffee cone filters but no *café moulu*.
Squeezed storefront springs joyous, ever more vacuous — luminous white.

Its Wonder breads green. Its Sealtest milks sour. Its slow decline
is a natural wretched marvel that keeps me returning, waking and dreaming.
Sell me some distrust, the fluke of the fact of desire, my open aching awe.

Priestly Demolition

It is construction season again
and my blood
flows through a leaf
caught in the centre of my chest.

A demolition is underway.
The lot beside the church is dirt, crane,
clatter. Men in white-and-black collar
scramble with wheelbarrow and ladder.

Pull down a rectory, board by board, in mud —
God-deigned hands in acts of destruction.
Montgomery Clift cassocks shift, as if
they walk on air, murder, tightrope rosaries.

Huge, swinging, an orange-armed mace.
The man pulling the stick shift, a master
of molestation. Around the site, black mice
scurry, eke out directions and psalms.

October is the month of flattening
images. Sky tossing tiny crosses of rain, like tin
jacks, between my boots. The only truth: Priestly,
a wooden name across a makeshift barricade.

This pew-on-pew row of posters
advertises a dirt lot.
A red and grey crucifixion
of summer. So long, September, sleep well.

The Keeper of Blueprints

My bridge is silver and high.
I've bridge-built for a quarter century — between
two white-twigged banks that I saw in a dream,
steep, shrouded with thumbprint petals. As you
might imagine, the financing has been complicated.
No one believes in my project. At night I eat
chocolate-caramels, Bridge Mixture, and weep.

Small details reiterate my failure,
even the slanted sun crisscrossing the floor,
the illusory bridgework of light.
I bridle my sorrow with sleep,
with green sheets and white briefs,
my brain an open briefcase, bursting
with the documents of image:

blue sky and gull shit,
Briggs-inspired calculations,
the decimals of high places,
a solemn brigade of automobiles
bright with the bend of exhaust.
                    Please please please please.
One simple line to cross.

Vanity of Vanities

Who wants to read about a Hell
that references other Hells?
That would take all the joy out of it.

Me, I'm the warm-glass-of-milk type,
stirred sweet with arsenic.
I like my Hell pure and simple.

When I was a child, I used the Bible
as a drum. All the other girls hid their tongues
behind their palms. But I played on.

On the very back pages, I'd written a name
inside a lopsided heart. *Who will mind?* I wondered.
Let him kiss me with the kisses of his mouth.

Depressed Women, Naked

Just one woman really,
her face a mustard stain
on the dull sheet of night.

She hangs like a crowbar moon.
If there are other women —
and this she doubts very much —

they wait in other rooms,
speaking a language of ash,
heads like urns, hips like spoons.

The House Across the Street

Your things move in, unpack
themselves late at night
in the lit window
while you are strangely absent.

The frame from the previous evening
is like a canvas undone
by a new colour.
Everything is laid out to dry,

the muddy choices you've made
on the far wall — sad paint, a set
of shelves with only a hammer
and a clock to hold.

Missing Notes

After midnight I awake
to sleep's frantic singing
& my mother's mad fiddle
the scratching of her fingers
& long lines of worried rhyme.

She untucks the corners
& opens the curtains.
She moves about the dark house
looking for things
we no longer own.

Something is missing
a string a pick a bow
a word a bit of memory
the dish & the spoon
the dog the baby.

I can still feel
her hipbones as handles
& the night cramped with stillness
as we all held tight.

Too old for this memory
& the bed too crowded
my father held my hand down the hall
back to my room closed the closet door.

Where is my father
in this dream? We are changing
places again & again
from darkness to darkness
a long yellowed hallway between us.

My mother drums her fingers
on the rooftops
& the rain stands at the window
looking out at her
its arms folded.

When I wake again I hear her
pulling old coats from closets.
She unwinds the cords
& vacuums up the night
a slow chaotic rhythm to her snores.

With Pennies for Eyes

The night hangs itself
like a bedsheet over the window frame
as I sit inside this painted box
like a jack pressed down.

Many people have lived
in this apartment before us.
When we make love
the dead are watching.

They have no television,
but they can't complain. For them,
time is different, morning never more
than a few hours away.

The dead can't eat ice cream or go to movies.
They have few options. They have only us:
you and your torn underwear,
me and my stretched black bra.

Our script is simple.
No betrayal, no amnesia, no anecdotes.
No captions. No commercials for bright
objects that will soon need dusting, repair.

There are only our shapes in motion.
You fold and unfold my body at the knees
as if opening and closing a music box
to make it play from the beginning again.

This is our theme.
Afterwards, you open the window and smoke,
blowing the grey air from your lungs
into the gnat-coloured night.

Riot at the Dollarama

There is a blood clot made of humans
in the long white aisle,
tremulous fluorescents and mellifluous
stink of cranberry votives, orange
knock-off Mr. Clean. Hand-gripped silver
baskets bumper-car semi-accidentally
into hips. There are no limits here,
not like at the Price Chopper.

Right now, the hot item
is skin cream, an herbal-silk fountain
retailing for eight dollars at Guardian Drugs.
No one can say for sure
if it will really stall your leg hairs' growth,
but there is a seven-dollar savings
and that is enough.

Stupid Poem

Don't get the wrong impression.
It's getting better here all the time.
With all the rock stars moving in,
there's a benefit concert every weekend.

Planning Tomorrow's Misery Today.
Soon we'll have roads and schools
and we won't have to walk
barefoot on gravel.

We'll have cars and money and manicures
like they do in Heaven,
and we won't have to look each other
in the eye sockets ever again.

III

a climax of dirt

For the People in Advertising

Night etches lines in strangers' faces. There's no pill for that.
Fear opens a bar and sells bitters to eucalyptus-breathed men.
Women wing by, wrapped in little pieces of yarn.
And you have your own sex, your own sadness, your own brand

of night. You make your bed with great deliberation.
Christ is your father, always standing over you,
prayers of chastity, blood-bright knuckles.
Like a sergeant, he tests the tightness of your sheets.

In the dark, a blond blossom of a woman lies down with you
and you pretend to be human. You could almost fool yourself,
sucking her fat hard toes as if they were grapes.
Love, distilled, into singular moments of reciprocity.

You can give. You are not exempt
from its power. You can leave your snapping fingers
in your desk drawer and go home
to find your heart still beating in your chest.

During the day, you wear hate like a scratchy sweater.
Happy hour starts at five, and you take yours alone,
parked on this swivel stool, your glass never empty.
The proprietor's joke clock shows nothing but 5's.

Your life plays out over top of you, silent purplish slide show.
The woman who's really writing a novel nods off into her drink;
the man with the controls clicks by too soon; *Bad design*,
someone says, but no one sees that you're hanging in air, flickering.

The small tick marks on the clock's face suddenly multiplied by 12,
and yours are also. Where is your woman now?
Vodka has its own smooth tongue,
quick and bloodless, like a nail through your cold blue veins.

Night forces itself through you, snap-stiff as a binder's rings,
holds you in place, carries you under its arm,
presses you, upright, into some small clean space
you will call your own until morning.

For Memory

We will not see the time we are living in
as time at all, but rather the end of all time.
In my mind you are thirty-six exposures

from one angle. You are the light going off.
My eye is the black bar that blinks
a segment of darkness between

your skin — your skin — your skin.
The slim repetitive parts of you
that age without my noticing.

You will always be seventeen.
You will always be twenty-seven.
The world will always be

pulling up its pants
in the damp cold grey of morning, ready
for another war.

Soft Ice Cream

In the smallest town the stillnesses fill
with crickets, the highway bright
with the dairy light menu gleaming
above the darkened counter in case
at this impossible hour
you might like to taste the trickle of raspberry
poured perfectly, curving down from
a rich creamy nipple, down into
a red and white paper boat,
pink plastic spoon standing upright.
And yellow lettering underneath —
choclat marshmalo btrscotch hot fudg strawbery
kiddie sm med lrg delux.

The ground at your feet is littered
with broken glass and bottle caps,
laughter flicked from a chained-down picnic table
to a crumbling parking block,
the tall tales of cigarette butts'
mouths since gone. And every breath
is an exchange you make knowingly
with the thick night air
that squats over you, nearly solid
with its whirring of insects and stars.
The spit in your mouth sours

beneath the candy cherry
of your own tongue.

If anyone were to ask the reason for this
you could only reply,
    Who is the sadness for?
Sadness has no reasons. Sadness is a luxury
of spare time, a piece of pie leftover,
the blueberry's skin caught between your teeth,
the black blear of happiness.
No one knows you here, still
you wish you could throw your head back
and burst into an instant jingle,
black out the light behind the glass with a stone,
pry up the foil ridge of the sky
and suck all the sweetness out.

Nothing Was Ever Going to Change

Meningitis nailed you down
— or the nurses did. Your wrists still ripe
with blueberries a week later.
Where are my glasses? the first thing
you say when you wake.
The second thing, *Where are my cigarettes?*

You keep holding Dad's hand
and I stand in the doorway.
I drink your apple juice. You don't want it.
The kind with the top peeled back.
The weight has come off you like old
wallpaper, half a strip still sticking.

In the dark driving home, the amber anxious bulb
of Dad sucking back tar. Sickness, another breath
we're all waiting to let out. Even Ross shuts up.
The night's gagging outside the car.
Two hours — Big Dipper in the sky. Cancer waits
down the road, its small bright consequential eyes.

Leftovers

The sky is a damp paper towel
laid over the world
to stop it from going bad . . .
And you are in the bowl
watching the morning light
obstructed by layers —
the walls of the city
sloping gently above you
so that the whole world lives
within the mouth of a constant yawn.

People in transit swim around you
with goldfish mouths.
Your boss gives you useless gifts
to keep you on-board
and you stumble home under
that grey six o'clock sky
watching the clouds for a break —
a place where the thick
rolls away, giving way
to oxygen and earnest light.

A Labyrinth of Pockets

My tenancy here will be brief.
On one side lying still.
The night is my father.
Sleep opens its mouth
and air cycles out.
I hold to the blanket,
each muscle a million.

Minutes migrate. From crown of skull
to soft scratchy parts. Here and here
and there. I will live only
in these eight inches of bed.
Sleep will lie with me
as if with a virgin, and neither of us
will make the first move.

The Pornography of Prime Time

You wake to find you've slept in again,
the light full of shadows and strange dreams.
Half-deaf, your helium head
rings with the acoustics of sleep.
You stumble through your life
like a strung-out teenager — dope-
diddled, pleasure like a dumb numb —
nodding your head
when you miss the question.

The day leaves too early,
like a boss who's always out the door
to important lunch meetings
though everyone jokes
she keeps a bottle in the top drawer.
Clouds through the window like the dark blue hem
of a coat flapping. The click of the door latch
the sound of freedom in a day agape with grey.
Work hard and you'll get ahead.

Supper eats you out of another twenty bucks,
and the country contemplates the cost
of a fuck, imaginary made-up lives, the stone-drone
silence of TVs parked in restaurants:
the world at war while people sit mouthing words.
Overhead smiles. The staff gives you change
without touching your hands.
You're that lonely guy at the end of the bar.
You never thought it would happen,

but here you are. Don't forget your hat
when you leave. You've only just begun
the long cold trek
into ordinary.

A Climax of Dirt

On Christmas day we stood on the grave
of the sky. The firmament was the colour of milk,
earth breast-white, trees exhaling snow.

Without warning, sound broke out of me
like animal. Electricity wailed from the top
of my shock, along my fingers —

the vibration of clutch.
A missing thing involuntarily sounded.
Stone at what it already knows.

Head letters, small symbols for breath and touch,
in past tense, one who now communicates
only with the carrion of rain,

enumerates at the doors of trees,
only touches in the way that shrubs
real the air I breathe.

You held my tears in your white peonies,
the sweetest kind —
hands, sad certainty of ants.

It was important that you were nothing
and said there, except your heartbeat
beneath your calm shirt beneath your noisy parka.

The world was waiting for turning
and we us-ed around and walked back into it, careful
of where we stepped.

Outside the cemetery fence, bright
cars engraved plumes of exhaust on the thoroughfare.
Fifty-year-old wreaths O-ing the atmosphere.

Joy was like a clowned-up blow,
begging us to throw
the first punch.

New Year's Eve

Perfume like a brand-new blank document.
The graveyard Christmas,
frozen, two hundred miles away.

Girls have a crisp laughter, like all the joy, all
the anticipation of a decisive starred sky —
presented for your perusal.

Under all the gloves tying their merry knots
on the hall table, you look for the pair
that will lead you home.

Two Minutes (one-hundred-twenty per hour)

The rain folds the night,
paper crackling
between its arthritic fingers.

We drive without talking,
without thinking,
the world around us an open mouth.

The wheels hold us, humming
over wet concrete.
The searching green-eyed glow of speedometer.

A billboard's bright face against the dark.
An exit sign.
We follow the arrows, read without reading.

Service centre like a space station,
we find our feet again,
unfold — lock up, fumble, walk, and float.

The air starched hard
against our teeth.
We carry out, and swallow sweet.

Tonight, tonight, tomorrow, tomorrow,
we go, slamming doors,
tiny teeth of a key kissing the ignition.

Between Road and Sky

I loved you that night I went into you
in a $22 motel in the middle of nowhere.
I watched light rise from your face
and hover in halos around the room:
on the door handle, and over the headboard,
above dusty lampshades
that had cast light down at the request
of thumbs and fingers that might never ask again —
that had flipped through the Gideon's Bible,
or quietly torn pages from the phone book
for the name of a place to eat,
the name of a friend in the next town.

I braced my knees against well-worn carpet,
pulled off mismatched blankets,
my hunting jacket and your jeans.
I went into you not expecting this light.
You made the sounds of a baby.
Your legs curled back and fingers opened.

Even while we slept I could hear the creak
of the bed like a cradle beneath us.
Outside, cars with their lonely people in the wind
came for us and moved away again.
Between the hollow noise of engines,
I rode your breath with wanting
to love you again and again, and only able
to dream of your skin
as a place where I lived
and died, abandoned in a wrinkled bedsheet map.
And in the morning from someplace far away
I could hear you singing.

IV

in the factory

In the Factory

The light burns always green in the factory where pain is produced.
The many hands that mould and file its edges, that pour its liquid
contents into trays and convey it from one set of eyes to the next,
shape it by rubbing each hard face smooth — sparking orange against
the wheel, all muddy compound crumbling clean, so to the bath of
chemicals, and dissolve in solvent — those same hands know it bet-
ter than any others — this bright instrument of manufacture, its
inherent quota like a stone, the crevices of its fluted sides, its leaden
hue this side of black — those same hands get a discount, lug it home
at Christmas, those same hands can hold it and say by their touch:

> this is a good pain, this is a bad pain, a defect pain, a sick pain,
> half-formed, without flourish, like the one I made first time I
> walked through those doors, like the uncast anguishes of tomor-
> row, pressed already into the small of my spine while I sleep,
> when all my sleeps become twisted, corrugated with the names
> of childhood friends I can no longer recall, and the thick dark
> coils of my mother's genitals the instant I was old enough to
> label them obscene in my mind, in its shamed corners where
> pains would grow into the faces of men, the stiff engraved souls
> that touched my palm like coins, went away and came back
> again, a pain less round than the others, one I don't even want to
> call my own, a pain without any dignity,
>   without silver or substance,
>   without a bit of shine,
>   and I could get you a hundred better
>   from any one of the bins out back.

Is it some dumb schmuck bent ogre-like, arthritic, tending to the dim arithmetic of production for an invention he knows will kill him, surely, slowly, in the end? A lawyer in a grey suit will send out bills for the truth — the affectation of inspections, a legal command: fix *what's wrong on the floor* — yet the triage of machinery is tacked up, still undone — *priorities priorities* — stamped with intention in a faceless man's office away from deaf lives who bleed on screws. . . . Someone will lose a hand over this, sever a digit to fast-pack that crate of pain. But factory workers don't suffer from insomnia, and the lawyer is already dead, heart clanging loud as that vice right over there, then still as the sink in the men's room, just like that, in one breath, a breath with the same songs as any other:

> *this is a pain worn so thin from rubbing against your chest you can see clear through it, like your father's old shirt just before your mother cut it to rags and he cursed her, throwing the scissors across the counter when he found it, a pain without opacity, without substance, without a muscle to carry it, something antique-faded, history-less, despite its new owners' attempt to love it, reeking of mould, a sold thing, a pain like a dull pencil, like the scratching of letters, like the tender mouths of mice who have eaten poison and borne it back to their holes in their intestines, plump, ready to burst, as gaping as the silence of offices at night, or the gun hidden in the top dresser drawer, like the strain of the family who need protection, the carefully folded bank slip,*

its simple unkind sets of plus and minus, tuition
and intuition, the pain the poor
carve with their eyes
just by looking at you.

If one moves from the factory floor to the offices, to the number-crunching management of pain — where the light is not green but ice-coloured, magnificent as hate, where the world is a paper ball batted about by interns beginning a quest to dress like their girlfriends' fathers, that old elusive drug whispering success in bathroom stalls, while the state-schooleds' workdays halt, time clock scoffing its flurried fill of cardboard dicks, and for those who are left — keeners, niggly with numbers, intimate with outcomes, five-point plans, inconsequential income — the caffeinated buzz of streetlights becomes the only signal for stopping, yet nothing stops the how-do-you-tally-emptiness, the résumé of 24-hour grocery glow, checkout girl's mad typing, a symphony for Lonely, not unlike one's own:

this is a pain that is never good enough, that punches the wall,
a pain of high-speed, of cellphones, of cars, and keeping up, that
is plastic, that is cash-only, that can be bought for 60 cents an
hour, a pain that is white, plays the market, multiplies itself ten-
fold, outgrows its owner's capacity to understand it, must leave
its owner behind, vacation alone, all-you-can-drink packages,
with no love in its love, hating itself all the more, buying its
memories in Duty-Free stores, a pain big enough to swallow

other pains — those of sweatshops, war, the needled flesh and
grey lesions of the homeless, the addicted, a tangle of stereotypes
and politics, a pain that attends church but does not pray, that
never knew what it wanted but did as it was told, a pain that only
meant to please

> *its father, who is dead now*
>> *and cannot be pleased,*
>>> *a lost pain, a pain that remembers,*
> *and pulls out its old tennis shoes, and runs and runs and runs.*

The factory where it originates is dazzling, clean, a tremulous glow in the night, your own emerald city. You can carry this pain proudly, hang it off your key ring, stick it magnetically to your fridge and let its edges curl, buy a frame for it and prop it atop your mantel, drink from it in the mornings, wear it upon your chest, turn it on and off in meetings or over awkward lunches with relatives or in-laws or former lovers, never mind that there are a hundred thousand dozens-upon-dozens exactly like it, boxed, opened, and set to line the shelves, it was designed especially for you for those moments, and it cost you nothing. This pain has been spell-checked, it is a reference letter singing your praises, it is a message without a date or subject line, a sender, or return address. It is guaranteed for life. Fold it and refold it, carry this letter in your pocket until letters go out of date, carry this poem in your pocket until poems go out of date.

V

letters to heartbreak

Dear Heartbreak,
         Who are you?

         Why do you have the eyes of my unborn twin,
my mother's most patronizing smile, the saunter
of my last love, and all my old clothes stitched together?
Why do you follow me in shopping malls
past toilet brushes and tank tops, general hardware,
comparing price tags, a pharmacy glow to your skin,
nipping away through the discount bins when I turn?

Dear Heartbreak,
     I think I know you.

          Didn't we lay together once in the dark
but scarcely touch — a-pulse with static,
each breath delightful, skittish, and cruel?
So dark I remember only your mouth: a year's worth
of kisses in its arsenal, your hair perfumed with smoke,
like autumn's brightest leaves,
gathered together, combusting into dust.

Dear Heartbreak,
   I tried to get in touch once before.

I meant to thank you for —
I'm dating your best friend now . . .
I can't believe it's been so long.
Even though we've never met . . .
How is your family? Career? Pet? Love life?
Bad news: a death to report. An illness. A sadness
beyond other sadnesses, one with my name on it
on a small sticker. Still thinking of you. *Please forward.*

Dear Heartbreak,
    I'm sending this via mutual acquaintance.

        All I ask is that you respond. The smell of you
still rises in my nostrils. My love wild-eyed
as an animal in taxidermy, mid-step, hollow,
excavated by silence, stuffed with sawdust.
I've seen you in passing cars (though you live far away now).
Between streetlights, your waiting face, distracted, sallow,
a strange yellow flame forged from shadow.

VI

poems for the wrong person

The Boy from the Theatre, the Excrement of Dogs

When we were together
we were always seeing ghosts.

The moon was the fullest and brightest
it had been in a hundred years.

I made love to you
but I was thinking of another.

Now you make love to another
and think of me.

We wandered the streets like two clowns, sleuthing
the stolen red circle of our one-ring show.

In our absence the little dog shat on the floor
and the crowd went home.

Out my window you saw something
that made you cry.

You lay back down next to me
under the cover of night.

I lay dreaming
that we were a thousand years old.

When I woke you were sunlight
and my heart was the cold colour of snow.

In the apartment below me
a spoon scraped the bottom of an empty bowl.

The Last Time I Saw You

(vii)

not her
but her bed.
not her
but her window from the street.

(xi)

a hatchback in a wet Virginia winter.
Joni Mitchell, Al Green.
answering machine. after work dinner special.
twenty-six and sick with lonely.
says the rain:
            always, always, always.
I drive and it drives,
final embrace a mouthful of sodden yellow leaves.

(vi)

suits suit him.

(ix)

he's crooning in the aisles with co-worker connection,
       baby, baby, baby, where did our love go?
       oh please don't leave me all by myself.
later his face will obscure with the fill between us
of third pints, sister's death still etched in his eyes.
night has longer fingers than we have: I dream him
all the way to Paris, some Pompidou platform
where we may — or may never —
kiss before awakening.

(xiii)

love's always got its fists up too early —
cowardly starts it but won't throw the first shot.
with breath like burnt matches,
       yeah and yeah and yeah and yeah —
and he is led away,
cursing and grateful, by another.
dark head bobbing its own blurred
ellipses . . .

(xv)

the man and his coat.
the man and his cigarette.
the man and his wife at home, unpresent,
present. departing woman
tucked away, missiled through the dark
in a bright yellow cab,
fare ticking.

(xvii)

mucking up the names
with drunken precision.

(xviii)

birthday theatre. well-costumed.
years like ribbons,
curled up on themselves.
stay pretty, stay pleasant, don't stay
longer than one should.

(xiv)

the shape of your skin when I have left it:

      blank page/screen. my beloved.
muscular breath, crepuscular collarbone,
body a bible of shadow.
history as long as the air.

The Night You Were Making Love to Me and Opened a Window in My Back to Fling a Bowl of Goldfish Out

                              Where even poems
are blind, and they sit waiting for someone
to lead them. The old dog with a snail for its heart,
its mouth full of chicken bones.
                         Where God
shakes a tambourine on the street corner
but there are only pennies. Tossed so quick
they drop, plinking, beyond the brim
of his bent black hat.
                              Where even the River Styx
is as thin and dry as licorice,
as laughable.
               Where I find myself finally, twisting,
on Sleep's tremulous tongue,
one of those other-dreamed
burnished fish,
long gone.

A Strategy for Escape

While the greatest poet on Earth was giving a reading
a stage door opened and shut again — loudly.
Eight hundred heard it and instantly knew
that the poor soul who had done it —
whether reporting to work mid-performance

covertly entering the back way or ineptly
propping the steel door wide
to solve some problem of backstage airflow
removal of equipment or garbage or letting it oopsy-slam
when stepping out for a quick well-deserved puff

or emergency-exiting (asthmatic hive-ridden swollen choking)
or simply forgetting let it go unchecked unlocked
to be jerked open by some stranger some lost undergraduate
— yes the brains between 1600 ears accepted:
that poor soul responsible would be fired immediately

would be turning in a badge clearing out
a desk drawer a locker of lists old snacks ticket stubs
a linty deodorant stick and broken luck charms
during the cigarette hour the cheek-kissing hour the slow after-show
hour of mislaid purses and scarves and trickled goodbyes.

The poet kept on reading as if nothing had happened
in the night-swell of fabric back there. . . .
In the aftermath the auditorium was its most silent most solemn
and by comparison the poet's poem nimbler
more lithe more musical more here more yes

until at least 50% of the brains between ears
began to seriously reconsider whether they could even guess
what poetry was and still another 20% reassessed
the quick dismissal of the unknown soul (but only briefly).
The poet who constituted a slim 0.125% mentally ambled

beyond that swift unseen door where it was surely still bright
or bright enough anyway in the city gleaming with noise gasoline
    and trees
with garlic and beer with the dusk plum perfume of passersby
this sudden grass-shorn desire to run — even as the voice went on
sticking — the poet was certain — like clamouring typewriter keys.

Faye's Tennis Courts

The fond sound that snow has filched,
stuffed beneath itself: the bounce
of fluorescent green, the whump of it,
netless court unoutlined.
Two — side by side, unmarked.
Plush white winter, a playground criminal,
protected by chain link. The half-knocked-down
history of a stone wall. The icon of a lion:
national bank glowing from the adjacent building's lobby.
And the traffic of Queen Street, tonight on mute.
You wrote, *Who plays here —*
in the middle of the city's mental institute?
a year ago, two, in a thirty-page poem
to which you diligently attend, but never show.

Instantly, all of this is yours,
all Queen, all Shaw, the barren boulevard, the intersection's
blinking lights, the bludgeoned spray nozzle
of an incapable graffiti bottle that has writ — then rewrit
more clearly — the name of an actor
upon shelter wall, ignorant parking stand.
The sad swollen faces of those who come and go
through whirling doors of Dylar and Largactyl.
The eldest of the trees and all their fallen leaves.
The shops and galleries on the other side
with white frames and silver outlines,
content seriously Chicago, NYC, magazine-thieved:
loving, uncertain, student hands affixing them
at midnight for tomorrow.

Everything is stolen — and returned, rallied to and fro.
Our breath, the night, the sidewalk's archives,
the courts themselves, their green waiting under grey,
the blond sun that is slow and sure in its arrival.

A Group of Empty Trees, Regularly Spaced

When I met you it was like that, like night in Ohio, which is as empty
a state (with faith) as any (all things are) other (possible), like the time
I found a truck of bees parked on the track between apple and pear

and my uncle walked clear through them, his skin crawling (and I)
with wings (was so). Then Dad (very). Then me (afraid). These insects
with power to peer deep in pockets, get stuck and sting, leave a body abuzz

with allergy, but they only flitted upon the surface of that thing that was
my skin, that is (if that girl) my (and I) skin (are still), and we walked on (the
    same)
marsh-tough until we found a stone where my great aunt used to sit

seventy years ago. And we (a grey) all (stone) looked (an ordinary) at it (stone),
budding from Bellefountain mud at the (back then) edge of a group of
    (recently) empty
(sold) trees. Then we climbed back through, twitchy for home (sold, too).

But I didn't know you then. I was just fourteen (if it is), gawkier than time.
It wasn't until (still) I met your skin (yours) that I remembered (and I think
    it is)
those craggy trees, growing downhill, half branches, half blossom,

in white and black (and all), rock-candy sticks, the smell of distilled
cider (I wanted), a voluble (to say) flatbed truck (was) in the path
with its (yes) postal box system (and yes) of patient and curious bees (again).

Mean Production

Can you condense a relationship, cram two or three years
into a summer by making love every day until your skin
splits with pain, only to find yourself still reaching, post-
midnight, toward the machinery of muscle and bones
humming well past quota? The productivity of intimacy.
The small white pocks of stars under his chin where you
know he was stung by a house of bees one jade summer.
The hipbones and thighs that know your smell by touch,
the blind single cells you remove with your hand with
one simple caress, that remove you from yourself and
tell you to beg to hold on. The woman with the clipboard
behind the door, taking inventory of your emotions as
you come — who called her in? Mean production and love,
what unfortunate partners. August has its lunchbox and
its timecard, a yellow smear of black ink, its hat pulled
low, so you don't notice when he slips out for cigarettes,
coffee, double, single cream. Love is the trigger of a gun,
innocent enough on its own, the last part to come down
your line, and you wait for it, grinning, your hands shaking
with expectation of ending this clumsy summer shift, its
sweat and sweetness, by putting together what you ought
to have seen was a shimmering vehicle for violence.

24 Hour Super Save

My three-man winter the coldest, longest moment. An igloo of blue
and white, this rented room above Lippincott and Bloor.
There are always ways to punish oneself momentarily —
the back entrance, a nightly climbing of alleyway fire escape,
a seesaw of icicle bones. Or skipping breakfast — twenty-four years,
I'm fuelled by nothing but bagel suppers, Paradiso Dark,
new Spicy Doritoes. One night in the bathroom my accidental heart
stops, wet-fingered, plugging/unplugging the light. My chest rings
empty, then blood-solid again. I sing-gasp. The mayor calls
in the army to remove the mountains in the street. The CN Tower gulps
clouds, swallows. Every sixty seconds, saliva-coloured elevators descend
its concrete throat. Every day my dog pisses on Central Tech. It's 4 a.m.
when the animal wakes me. We flannel-walk. She, producing steam
from her yellow fur. Me, an impulse apple in ungloved hand. Its red skin.
I have stooped to this: I eat while she shits. How terribly hungry,
how trembling I am. Unseen in the raw night, Temporality yanks the leash.

Swivel Chair

In full attack mode
in a swivel chair
you had lugged out

maybe not for that purpose
since it was my idea,
but it sufficing nonetheless

for a balcony beer-bottle falter,
we banged teeth,
eager 4 a.m. bones,

as the cat
with the punched-in face
struck its claws

down the beams on the other side
of our mid-air,
dark-treed moment —

our eyes flicked open and closed,
faces nudged through
one another, your tongue a solid wall

until
I suggested we move indoors,
the whole thing over in an instant,

called off,
as if logic were a doorway
we could step through.

For a few seconds out there,
the beating thing
behind your breasts,

which flushes blood
throughout you, hung among the trees.
And in my mind it still

hangs among trees. Twelve hours
later, are the echoes
light through leaves?

I am eight blocks farther
from you than then, and soberer,
ashamed of dwelling

on the tenderness that skulks in,
flexing its tiny soft-and-mean,
where it is unwanted.

Portraits of Fruit

(1)

The light of oranges
in your hands in the morning.
The wet spark of breaking.
With fingernails for knives,
you pry out half smiles
from aching yawning sections,
pale thin veins.
Peel the skin slowly, and then, let it fall
white side up on the blue
willow plate. And me —
when you go you leave me
a smeared sun behind my skin,
dabs of marmalade and margarine.
I pour an English Breakfast Tea
and clink the cupsides to crack
the silence with a spoon.

(2)

Perhaps you are mispainted.
That orange, opened bright as a scar.
We could not have begun that way.
Weren't you more like grapes
in summer? I remember
you beside the arbour
pulling a handful from the vine, rolling one
into my open mouth. I bit bitter-
sweet and you said
they were for making
wine. When you put your tongue
against my teeth
I felt the night crackling
under our feet,
fallen seeds and stems.
On the backs of our arms,
the buzz of mosquito stars.

(3)

In autumn, again the light
has fallen. I may forget
the smell of you sleeping —
the sweetness of sun, your sunken breath
replaced by leaves and wind,
and skin, by the skin of trees.
Sin will be dyeing her hair for a new season.
If you sleep through the after-
noon you will miss me
on a timeless whirled
scent of apples
and lost gardens, cellophaned bouquets
in plastic baskets.
I will be waiting for you
at the corner market. I will be waiting.
I pluck an apple from the bin
and begin
to look for spots.

Night Undresses

Night is when underpants come off.
The white of day is pulled down slowly.

In the next room you spit in the sink.
The world, a worry flushed into sleep.

Condensation puckers outside surfaces
and stubble shadows the room.

My body is a bird ducking its head.
The light, a knuckle curved into a crevice.

Night is for tea whistles
in otherwise silent structures.

For unsteeped thoughts to strain
into astonished cups.

For mouths to open with steam and seal
beneath a dark floating skirt of sky.

Poem for the Wrong Person

Of the hundreds of thousands
of nights to be, we sleep against each
other, just one. Detached as sea
gull feathers, these kneaded skin
covers. When you recollect
me, I am not myself. Years will beat,
rub, and water-polish the idea
smooth: an instant of keeping,
a collapse of terms,
my mouth a paper boat in the dark.

We drift toward the dream
of a flock of birds floating
in the tree beyond the screen,
a song of silence swallowed
in last breaths. Between
we wait for the blink
that closes ceiling cracks and corners
of mouth, the spaces where
one of us is awake for one more breath
across the whirlpooled white pillowcase.

That moment is not yours
as it funnels to the grey outside the window.
Last breath is held
in holes in the screen —
the ending you will never see.
Only the sound of sky
echoed from notquite corners and treetops
as syllables dissolve beneath
the weight of sleep surrounding.
I've forgotten who I am writing.

The Week John Ditsky Died

In Detroit, fifty officers have a warrant
to seek his remains. Hoffa, that is,
on the front page; Ditsky's in the back.

A man of crime is exhumed. A man of letters
laid to rest. Delivered via e-mail and old acquaintance,
the paper's smudged weight sits upon screen, illuminated,

uncanny, popping with ads for its own Classifieds.
The Death Notices yawn with tulips.
Visitation is for an 11 a.m. already passed.

The body, cremated.
The New Steinbeck Society of America receives
the idea of flowers.

A search returns
an old poem lingering online, sexual, insistent, alive,
still singing the languor of May and some yearless first day of June:

plant me, plant me soon.

In Windsor, a bridge of pigeons,
a river of tankers and student drunkards,
pursuits of Steinbeck and Schlitz.

Ten years ago. That year we were all boys
and me. Ditsky instructed on the proper use
of four-letter words — *perhaps the more common verb*

here, the one that starts with C —
gently, precisely, as if working
with gloves and pincers.

In Toronto, the boys of a nameless high school
play three Frisbees across the street, zing
the thin white discs over traffic and me, with ease.

Concrete under concrete sky, I walk, because walking
is what you do when there is nothing else to be done.
When you are still young enough to feel

even a distant death. At the mouth of Close Ave.
and the Lucky Lotto vegetable stand, an old woman
hunches, gathering

individual green beans into her palm. One by one,
she selects them, a small packet of sticks, binds them
with finger and thumb.

The Thing Defines Itself

I am a soul in the world: in
the world of my soul the whirled
light / from the day
— from "The Invention of Comics,"
Amiri Baraka (LeRoi Jones)

The sound of sky is the sound of sky
reflected on the pavement,

the light that blinks,
the open image flung from our window.

The word is night,
the word that rises to your lips
is night, the word of the thing
it is, itself, is night
and the sound is
coarse and shimmering
as fallen leaves beaded with rain
and night.

That is all.
Night is night.

Night is night. You say it, I swallow it,
the sound, the long night Longing slips
out of its dark, old hand of lines.
The sugar-quick flick your voice pulls
slow through me, flickers high
out the other side as if you might
slip into the thing you define, small body full
of the word, repeating its meaning.

And my ears full
of reading its hearing.

Your voice is the lid
on the lighter you grip
between your fingers and thumb
click click, the clasp you open and close
for its opening-closing,
for no other meaning but this —
click its opening,
and click its closing.

The sound of you is the sound of you
shivering under the click click

of words and rain
in the night, is night, is night.

Notes

"Songs for the Dancing Chicken" draws inspiration from the films of Werner Herzog, with the exception of "Herzog's Other Shoe," which takes its inspiration from a short documentary by Les Blank, *Werner Herzog Eats His Shoe* (1980), and references Errol Morris' full-length film *Gates of Heaven* (1980). In a friendly bet meant to incite Morris to finish his first film, which was about a pet cemetery, Herzog promised to eat his shoe upon the film's completion. With much ceremony, Herzog held true to his promise, as documented by Blank.

The poem "Heart of Glass" references the Herzog film of the same title (1976). "New Rats" is based on his movie *Nosferatu* (1979). According to the Paul Cronin biography *Herzog on Herzog*, the rats used in the film were white lab rats and were dyed — in an elaborate process — for effect. "Sergeant Brown" draws on *Grizzly Man* (2005); "The Conquistador of the Useless," *Fitzcarraldo* (1982); "Even Dwarfs Started Small," the film of the same name (1970). "The Boat in the Tree" is inspired by the story behind *Aguirre: The Wrath of God* (1972), in which workers engaged in the difficult task of constructing and hoisting a boat thirty metres up a tree. The poem purposely exaggerates.

"Song for the Dancing Chicken" references *Stroszek* (1976), as does "For Werner Herzog" and sections 7–12 of "Double-Double and Hell on Earth." The chicken in the scene that ends the film was professionally trained to defy its natural abilities, learning to dance without reward for fifteen seconds rather than three so that Herzog could get the length of the shot he felt was necessary. In the *Stroszek* commentary, when the chicken comes onscreen, Herzog says, "Now

I think I shouldn't talk over this scene here, the chicken. It's just too good. No more comment. Full stop."

The author is grateful to Mr. Herzog for his films, and to his production company for permission to print the image from *Stroszek*. More information on Herzog and his work can be found online at www.wernerherzog.com.

The poem "Better Hell" includes reference to the poem "The Prodigal," which is by Charles Simic from his book *Hotel Insomnia*, and is re-imagined here.

The poem "For a Labyrinth of Pockets" draws its title from a line of prose in Vladimir Nabokov's novel *Bend Sinister*.

The poem "A Group of Empty Trees, Regularly Spaced" draws its name from a phrase put forth by Fran Lebowitz on what Chekhov's *The Cherry Orchard* might have been called if there were no such thing in the world as food. This poem has nothing to do with either Lebowitz or Chekhov.

Earlier versions of some these poems appeared in the following magazines: *Crash*, *Event*, *Fireweed*, *Queen Street Quarterly*, *subTerrain*, *Taddle Creek*, *This Magazine*, *The Walrus*, and *Windsor ReView*.

Songs

for publisher Jack David; editors Michael Holmes and Stuart Ross; and all those who work at ECW Press for font choices, serial commas, publicity magic, mailing labels, and much, much more;

for Don Sedgwick, Shaun Bradley, and all at TLA;

for Di Brandt and Kevin Connolly for their generosity; Stephen Cain; John Ditsky, whose quiet nods had a lasting effect; Dave Dyment for "Herzog's Other Shoe"; Faye Guenther, who knows tennis courts better than I do; Maggie Helwig, Bill Kennedy, angela rawlings, Damian Rogers, and the Scream in High Park festival (a scream for them, not a song); Dawn Lewis and Rebecca McClellan; Kitty Lewis, Liz Martin, and Mary Newberry for their smiles; Ray Robertson; Daniel Robinet; Conan Tobias for so many reasons; Rhea Tregebov, who taught me the word *enjambment*; Darren Wershler-Henry for lemon gin; Zoe Whittall; Julie Wilson; and Rachel Zolf, who recognizes lost chickens;

for Brian Joseph Davis, who dragged me to see *Aguirre* at age nineteen

— a thousand songs.